A DAILY DEVOTIONAL

ONE DAY
AT A
TIME

E. L. MYLES, JR.

DAY ONE

HE LOVES YOU

1 Samuel 1:1-5

*We live in a day and time in which we measure ourselves
and our value- by what we have...*

Often, we treat those with more possessions than we have, better than those who seem to have less than we do. Despite our flawed way of thinking, I am forever grateful that God continues to see our potential, even with our problems. In the first book of Samuel, chapter one, verses one through five, the text narrates the life of a man named Elkanah. Elkanah had two wives; their names were Peninnah and Hannah. Peninnah (Elkanah's second wife) had many children, which many in their society deemed a blessing and a woman of high esteem. Hannah, Elkanah's first wife, was barren and unable to conceive a child for well over a decade into their union. According to Jewish law, Hannah's inability to conceive, allows her husband to take on another wife- which is how Peninnah entered their household. Despite Hannah's infertility, Elkanah continued to love his wife, treating her with the utmost respect- even doubling her portions, after making his sacrifice at Shiloh. Remaining steadfast in prayer, Hannah's prayers were eventually answered, and God opened up her womb, allowing her to give Elkanah an abundance of heirs. Despite her setbacks, she remained grateful. Let this be a lesson that there should come a time in all of our lives when we merely thank God for simply loving us. We should thank God for looking beyond our shortcomings, situations, and bad habits while He continues to grant us with His favor.

*Today, take some time to reflect and just say:
"Thank you" for being loved by God is a beautiful thing.*

DAY TWO

BLESSED TO BE A BLESSING

1Samuel 1: 11

God will always give you more than you ask for...

Many of us often ask God to bless us daily. At times, our requests are very specific- "God, may I have this, God may I have that?" Most of our desires are aimed at bettering our personal lives- especially our material needs. In spite of our continued appeals to God for more, I've personally come to the realization that God relinquishes blessings to those that *He* can trust will BE a bigger blessing to others. Every blessing that we receive from God is also meant to be a blessing in some form or fashion to others. Make a conscious decision today, that the future blessings that you receive will not stop with you; but will be passed onto others. Ask yourself these questions: Can God trust you with a blessing? Are you able to look beyond yourself and bless others in need? Are you able to be the vessel that God has called His people to be? I hope so.

During times like these,
you never truly know why God has chosen you to be of service.
That same blessing that you share,
may one day be returned to you tenfold.

MOMENTS OF MEDITATION

DAY THREE

APPRECIATE THE PREPARED

John 1:15

Appreciation is one of the simplest forms of kindness...

We will never fully understand and grasp exactly what our ancestors experienced for us. Often times, we overlook or under appreciate the many sacrifices and valiant efforts made for us on their behalf. When dealing with life's hiccups, it is important to remember that while difficult, it will never compare to what those before us experienced. Had they not experienced the trials and tribulations of life- our life would be slightly unbearable. Imagine our life had our grandparents not experienced raising kids, attending school, or managing life's day to day stressors. Imagine not having anyone to guide us or tell us how they did it! Life would be pretty hard if not paved by those that came before us.

Today, take some time to appreciate those that prepared the way for us. Simply put, we are merely following in their footsteps. For, one day someone will be following in ours.

MOMENTS OF MEDITATION

DAY FOUR

LIVE RIGHTEOUS

Psalms 5: 12

Begin your morning thoughts with your goal in mind...

It seems as if we live in a day and time where our life is so important that we actually expect God to fit into our schedules! We as people are so consumed with time, that we actually live by calendars, alarm clocks, and planners- often expecting God to schedule Himself into our chaotic lifestyles. In our haste, I wonder how many of us have actually wondered if He would just- become, rather than fit? Let me explain. Instead of penciling Him in, could He become our schedules? Could He become our lifestyle? Could He become our life? No matter how you look at it, favor from God is always connected through faithfulness. If God became **OUR** priority, with us fitting Him into our everyday life, we would surely find the favor that we seek. If you want the favor of God, YOU have to be faithful in making time for Him. Ask Him to become your lifestyle. Ask Him to become your life. If you want the favor of God, you have to be faithful to Him. Your continued faithfulness will certainly reveal favor that will overwhelm you with joy.

Remember, we always make time and room for things we feel are important to us. Make room for God and stop expecting Him to just fit in.

MOMENTS OF MEDITATION

DAY FIVE

BE ACCOUNTABLE

Psalms 6

Accountability begats peace- if you allow it...

At some point in every person's life, there comes a time in which one must take full responsibility for their own actions. Taking responsibility for our own actions, words, and decisions renders us the ability to become closer to God. This self-awareness causes us to recognize our actions and how they fail to align with the actions necessary to enter the Kingdom of God. In the sixth division of Psalms, David's sins are revealed, provoking the wrath of God. David had to make a decision- to do the right thing- confessing his sins and awaiting mercy from God. Before mercy, grace, or deliverance can be fully appreciated, as in David's story, accountability has to take place. David had to consider the consequences of his sins, and how his life would end up if he continued down a path of unrighteousness. Many times, we want to make excuses for our actions, but we shouldn't. Our only aim in sight is to please God. In fact, excuses don't excuse our actions- they simply make room for self-acceptance and a continuation of the same types of behavior.

Today, I implore you to make a conscious decision. Make the decision to be accountable for all of your actions. Once you've made that decision, you will fully appreciate the mercy, grace, and deliverance of God.

MOMENTS OF MEDITATION

DAY SIX

SOME THINGS HAVE TO CHANGE

Matthew 9: 15 - 17

Change your ways and watch how your life prospers on God's path...

Often times, we make our life far more complicated by trying to do things *our* way when in all actuality- we know that God's way is not only *right*, but the best. When we continue doing things our way, we usually end up taking the longer, more painful route. If for once, we conformed to God and followed His plans, our lives would be far less complicated and far more prosperous. The fact of the matter is this: if we really want God to pour out His abundant blessings upon us, we have to begin to make preparation for it. God will not conform to us, as we are simply humans made in His form. Instead, we have to be transformed for Him. Our transformation can take place in many forms. It can happen by change of attitude. It can happen by change of habits. It can happen by changing your mindset. The best transformation that we can make is to give in and listen to God and follow His way. In order for God to pour into you, an internal change must first take place. Starting today, I challenge you to make one change that allows you to follow God's instructions. Change something that you know needs to be changed immediately and watch how God fills the voids within your life.

Keep in mind that change is inevitable;
personal growth is optional- it's your choice.

MOMENTS OF MEDITATION

DAY SEVEN

DON'T GIVE UP

Psalms 13

Everything appears to be impossible, until it's actually done...

There are many times in our lives when we find ourselves frustrated at our journey. During those times, we find ourselves exhausted and ready to throw in the towel. Our ambition lessens, frustration not only increases- but it becomes the norm. We find ourselves completely exhausted and short on the patience we desire from God daily. If that wasn't enough, this decrease in motivation usually occurs when you are really trying to do your best to obtain your goals! Yet, it seems like everything that can go wrong, has and does. Everyone is succeeding- even your enemies seem to be enjoying their life to the fullest. So, what exactly should one do when this happens? DON'T GIVE UP! This is the point in your journey that God has you right where He wants you. He knows that you feel weak, but He doesn't want you to give up! Our strength comes from Him. Whenever we are weak- He is strong and mighty. He doesn't want us to throw in the towel- He wants us to persevere! Keep praying. Keep pushing. Keep smiling. Keep serving. We experience our blessings and breakthroughs during our weakest points!

Be consistent in your self-growth, for your journey is yours to write.

MOMENTS OF MEDITATION

_____

_____

_____

_____

_____

_____

_____

_____

_____

_____

_____

_____

_____

_____

_____

_____

_____

_____

_____

_____

_____

_____

DAY EIGHT

TRUST IN GOD

Proverbs 3: 5

I will Trust the Lord with ALL thine heart...

It sounds so simple, yet, sometimes it can be so difficult for us to put our trust in God. Many times, the thing that keeps us from fully trusting God, is fear. Fear is not only an emotion- it's also a perception that one experiences when feeling or sensing danger, a threat, or harm. Fear often drives us from experiencing the blessings God has in store for us because we've failed to trust in Him. When we fail to trust God, we are not only letting ourselves down- but we are hindering our own personal growth. We as people actually fear that God won't come through for us, when in actuality- He has never let us down. We fear that He won't fulfill our desires in the time frame we feel we need them, when in retrospect, we know that He's an on time God. We fear that we will be let down, but we know that He has never failed us. I have personally learned that if I can trust a chair to hold me, without checking it out before sitting down, I can definitely trust the creator of the heavens and earth.

Trust God to take care of you and
you will certainly experience more peace within your life.

MOMENTS OF MEDITATION

DAY NINE

BE SATISFIED

Psalms 17

He has NEVER let us down and He never will...

Many of times we've found ourselves caught up in the moment of need. Not necessarily the moment of needing anything, but the moment of wanting more than we need. For some reason, we desire many worldly possessions- mostly things we don't necessarily require- despite our wants remaining completely fulfilled by Him. We mostly demand material items just to be boastful, or just to have the ability to compare them to the possessions of others. If we were truly honest with ourselves, we would acknowledge that we do not deserve everything that we have. I often imagine just how God must feel when we continue to ask for more. Does the word selfish come to mind? He continues to give and give- yet we fail to even thank Him for the simple things- like waking us up in the morning. Why is it so hard for us to be satisfied? Why not be thankful for the multitude of possessions we already own? Why not show gratitude for the myriad of blessings that He bestows on us daily? We are truly blessed and favored every time He allows us to see another day and experience the simple pleasures of life. We must learn to live our lives satisfied. Satisfied, not just with what God has already done for us- but satisfied knowing that He also blocked things from happening to us.

Remember, in all things give thanks...Be satisfied.

MOMENTS OF MEDITATION

DAY TEN

THE BLESSING IN OBEDIENCE

John 9: 6 - 7

Obedience is an ingredient to success...

Have you ever heard the saying, "You ask too many questions?" When I was a child, the adults in my life would often say that to me. It wasn't until I gained wisdom and matured, that I understood exactly what they were trying to teach me when they used that statement. The adults in my life weren't telling me to remain quiet or belittling me to hush up, they were actually communicating a message to me. The message was simple: "just trust me." Like curious children, we often get in the way of our blessings by asking God far too many questions. We also confuse ourselves by trying to figure out how God is going to do something. Imagine us, questioning God! We actually sit in wonderment wondering exactly when God will fulfill a need. There's really no need to worry or wonder. In the scripture it instructs us to trust in the Lord. All we have to do is trust and obey. I encourage you to obey God today and watch how blessings are bestowed upon your life.

Obedience will open your eyes to a world made custom for you.

MOMENTS OF MEDITATION

DAY ELEVEN

YOU CAN'T STOP ME!

Mark 10: 46 - 52

Be ye steadfast...

Many of us have yet to receive all of the blessings that the Lord has in store for us. We haven't received the half of those blessings because in some cases, we have allowed others to talk us out of receiving them. Let me explain, there are many of us that have been so close to our destination but have simply allowed others to convince us that our GPS is wrong. We listen to the "back seat" driver that instructs us to go another route- when God should be directing our journey. I've come to the realization that people do not mind you being blessed, just as long as you don't receive your blessings before them! God has and will always be in the blessing business. He will never run out of blessings for anyone. He has room to bless us all- we just need to remain steadfast and patient until it's our turn. I dare you to make the decision today that allows you to receive your blessings and be happy for others receiving theirs. Make the decision that nothing or nobody will stop you from receiving all that God has rationed out just for you.

What He has in store for you, is ONLY for YOU!
Stay ready and steadfast.

MOMENTS OF MEDITATION

DAY TWELVE

ORDER MY STEPS

Genesis 16: 2

Order my steps dear Lord...

Everything that sounds good, may not always be of Godly sentiment. Many of us often seek good advice to assist us while navigating life's ups and downs. We will listen to doctors, therapists, close family members, and friends to make sure we are doing what's right. I often wonder how many of us seek true Godly advice before starting a new journey or attempting to solve a problem? I have learned that as a follower of God, everything that I do should have God's approval. However, I've also learned that many of us fail to seek God's advice because we've already established within our hearts what it is that *we* want to do. To make matters worse, not only do we fail to seek His approval- we then do as we see fit and still are bold in asking God to bless it! Perhaps we should seek God's advice first, allowing Him to order our steps. Once we start doing that- every decision we make will already be blessed and aligned with His will. Think about how much time you have wasted dealing with bad decisions that you've made in the past. Think about how simpler life would have been if we simply made decisions based on God's advice.

Today, take some time to make sure your path
aligns with God's path for your life.

MOMENTS OF MEDITATION

DAY THIRTEEN

LET GOD GUIDE YOU

Genesis 22: 8

Where He provides; He also guides...

God has consistently done everything He has stated that He would. Without fail, His promises have arrived on time, often exceeding our expectations. Despite our shortcomings and trust issues, He has never left us without. We often times become unsettled or nervous because we're trying to figure out God's moves. We're not sure how He'll do it, let alone when. We ask God for so much, yet we fail to trust that He will provide all of our needs. I have come to realize that I don't necessarily need to know how or even when He is going to do what I've asked of Him. I'm simply grateful that He will continue to fulfill my needs- even my wants as He sees fit. When you are waiting for God to provide a need- be patient. When you begin to feel that nervous energy come over you, or you feel unsettled- stop and remind yourself that if He said it, He will definitely do it. There's an old saying that says: "He may not come when you want Him; but, He's always on time" and that saying is still just as true today.

Today, take some time to Trust that the Lord will provide.

MOMENTS OF MEDITATION

DAY FOURTEEN

JUST A PRAYER AWAY

James 4: 2

You have not, because you ask not...

Most of us have desires of the heart that we've never shared with anyone else. The desire to be wealthy, healthy, famous, or just loved in a manner that we want. Many of these desires fail to come to fruition. While we are equipped to receive these requests- and we often put in the effort for them- we still fall short inheriting our deepest desires. Why are these desires not fulfilled? It's simple: we haven't asked God to fulfill them. Ask yourself this: how many times have you desired something and without going to God- your first thought is how YOU are going to make it happen? When, in reality, your first thought should be, is this YOUR will Lord? Let God be your guide. Let Him be the designer of your hearts desires.

Today, instead of trying to make things happen on your own, commit to asking God for your hearts desires and let His will be done.

MOMENTS OF MEDITATION

DAY FIFTEEN

HE SAW THE BEST IN ME

Mark 5:1-8

Do you see what I see?

Many of us have been identified or categorized by our present situation or material items. People often times identify us by our possessions (Oh, that's Jim- he drives the Mercedes, Or that's Tameka with the two kids). They'll even go further to identify us by our titles (doctors, teachers, lawyers, accountants) just so they can measure the amount of respect we should have. Regardless of our possessions and titles, we should never allow those items to define who we are. We are more than our worldly possessions. We are more than the titles we wear for our employers or companies we own. We are children of the most-high God. That is the ONLY title that matters. When you look at yourself on the mirror, see yourself as God sees you. See yourself as a creation of the creator. Visualize yourself in HIS likeliness. Never allow your possessions to possess you. Instead, step into the light and become what you were created to be.

Remember, we are made in HIS image!

MOMENTS OF MEDITATION

DAY SIXTEEN

TO WHOM MUCH IS GIVEN, MUCH IS REQUIRED

Matthew 25: 14 - 30

*The "gift" that God bestows upon you
should also be shared with others...*

I have come to discover that the enemy of faith is fear. Many of us fail to operate in the full capacity of our faith because we allow fear to control us. I have come to realize that the offspring of faith is reward. One concept I realized after reading this scripture is that even though the Master gave a different amount of talents to each servant. The Master viewed all the talents as a few things. However, the servant that was given one operated in fear. He never realized that his one talent was equal to the other servants. Don't allow fear to obstruct the perception of your gift. Today, remind yourself that I may have plenty. I may have a little, but, at least I have! Be faithful with your gift.

*Today, remind yourself that you have plenty of gifts
and talents from God. No matter the size of your gift or talent-
be faithful with what you have.*

MOMENTS OF MEDITATION

DAY SEVENTEEN

BE CREATIVE

Genesis 1:1

Creativity doesn't strike at the perfect moment...

The Bible says that we are created in the image and likeness of God. One of the first things that God did was create. He created to please Himself and to be a blessing. Because you are created on His likeness, there is a creative gene inside of you. Many of us ignore our creative side or talk ourselves out of using it. Whether it's because of finances, opportunity, or procrastination. Don't allow anyone or anything to keep you from being creative. It doesn't matter if it's starting a business or planting flowers in your yard. Tap into your creativity. Your creation may just be the blessing that someone else is waiting for.

Today, allow your creativity to become a reality.

MOMENTS OF MEDITATION

DAY EIGHTEEN

THIS IS FOR YOU

2 Kings 4: 1 - 7

Serving others, is the rent we pay for our time here on earth...

Psychologists have suggested that over 80% of our stress is often caused by other people's situations. This means that many of us take on other people's problems as if they're our own. This is a clear depiction of what happened on Calvary. While other people are eating, you are fasting on their behalf. While they are out having fun, you are at home praying on their behalf. You made them a priority. You made up in your mind that you were created for this. You were created to be the vessel that God uses to help someone else- not take on their problem- but help them find a solution to their problems. As we often see our family and friends experience life, God calls us to be the intercessory they need while on their journey. When we follow God's directions, praying and fasting for others, we are doing His work. We are being the vessel that He wants us to be in the life of others. Always remember that YOU were created for this. You heard me correctly, you were created JUST for this role in someone else's life. You were created to be the vessel that God will use to help someone else.

I know you may be thinking,
"well who is going to be there for me on my journey, as I am for others"? My response... God. He's never left us alone. Even when we're working on other's- He is with us and working through and for us.

MOMENTS OF MEDITATION

DAY NINETEEN

NOT EVERYONE HAS TO BE IN THE KNOW

2 Kings 4: 26 - 37

Your secret is safe...

The mistake that many of us have made (including myself), is that when we experience difficult times in our life, we either keep it to ourselves, allowing it to build up or we tell the wrong person- which can be disastrous. While trying to be private and keep our problems personal, this also prevents the right person from helping you. However, telling the wrong person your personal thoughts and journey can be a hindrance because they are not the right person to confide in and will not possess the tools to help you. I believe that when you experience difficult moments in life, the best course of action is to ask God to order your steps. When we allow God to order our steps and guide us through storms, we are trusting Him to do as He always does- and that is take care and protect us. Sometimes, what stands between you and your breakthrough is a connection with the Lord. When we trust and allow Him to guide us, we remain connected with Him. Not only will He guide us, but He will connect you with the right individuals to assist you on your journey.

Today, ask the Lord to order your steps
and connect you with the right person.

MOMENTS OF MEDITATION

DAY TWENTY

GUARD YOUR HEART

Provers 4: 23

Positive thinking is a contagious...

The heart is one of the major organs located within your body. Not only does it supply blood to all areas of the body, it also creates the rhythm in which our body functions. The brain is another organ that our body needs. Processing information, making decisions, and housing our mind are all stored within our brain. Often times the heart and the mind are synonymous in meaning. Therefore, what we allow to penetrate our heart, will also impact how we think. It can impact how we live our lives and even how we respond to situations. Today, make a conscious effort to guard your heart from anything negative. Whether it be the music you listen to, the conversations that you have, or the shows that you watch. Always guard your thoughts from the negativity within the world.

Today, take time to prevent negative thoughts
to accumulate in your mind- in doing so, you will soon discover
how positive situations will surround you.

MOMENTS OF MEDITATION

DAY TWENTY-ONE

IT'S NOT TOO LATE

Hosea 14: 1 - 9

Repent...

One of the greatest moments in my life happened when I repented my sins to God. This was the exact moment that made me realize just how much God really loved me, so much so that He gave me the opportunity to recognize and acknowledge my wrongs. He also allowed me the opportunity to apologize and turn from my sins to the path of righteousness. I hope that someone reading these words will see that the greatest reward for you, is this opportunity to repent. None of us are flawless! We have all had a few moments in our life that require repentance. Don't miss your moment of redemption from sin. Your moment of restoration presents itself every day you wake. Ask God to place your feet on the path of righteousness, for His namesake. It's not too late.

Today, take some time to review your life. When was the last time that you repented to God? It's never too late to do the right thing.

MOMENTS OF MEDITATION

DAY TWENTY-TWO

RESTORE ME

Mark 8: 22 - 25

Lord, do it again...

There are many things that I love about the Lord. For starters, I love His patience, I love His faithfulness, I love His compassion, and I love His mercy. The virtue that I truly appreciate about Him the most, is His ability and willingness to restore. Most of us, if not all, have made mistakes in life, have been bad, or made selfish decisions. Despite all of this, the Lord was still merciful enough to make us whole again. What continues to amaze me- is His willingness to restore us- which He continues to do again and again. I don't know about you, but I am very grateful that He touched me again. I am very grateful for His never ending love and his continual restoration- despite my sins. Today, ask the Lord to do it again. Ask Him to restore you again, ask Him to heal you again, and finally- ask Him to give you peace again. If you ask Him, I believe that He will do it- over and over again.

Today, take some time to ask God for a full restoration over your body.

MOMENTS OF MEDITATION

DAY TWENTY-THREE

A BLESSING IN BELIEVING

Mark 5: 36

It's in His hands...

I've discovered that many of our problems seem far worse than what they really are. This usually happens because our faith is shaken- and not unmovable as it should be. The real issue is not the circumstances of our problems at all. The real issue is actually the unknown outcome. I've also realized that if God always told us how things would end, or when they would happen- there would be no need for us to possess a strong faith in Him. The main purpose of faith is to substantiate what you hope for- yet cannot see. When we pray it's generally for two reasons. The first reason- because you have a hope, a need or a reason to believe. The second reason that we pray is because whatever challenge we're experiencing- we know that we can't conquer it on our own. When we believe and have faith in God, we are blessed to have the responsibility of what happens out of our hands. We then place those problems and situations in the hands of God.

Always trust in God. Always believe in God. Always remain steadfast in your faith. All will work out- according to His plans.

MOMENTS OF MEDITATION

DAY TWENTY-FOUR

PEACE

John 14: 27

Peace be unto you...

Throughout the many years that I have been blessed to live, there have always seemed to be a void or empty space within my life. Despite those voids and empty spaces, I still continued to receive many blessings from God, I still continued to exercise my gifts from God, I still continued to possess many valuables, and I even became accustomed to a certain lifestyle. I've often appeared happy- yet there was always a sense of emptiness surrounding me. Through long periods of self- interrogation, I finally realized that the one thing I was missing was peace. Not a sense of comfort- like knowing that all of the bills are paid, there's food in the refrigerator, or money in the bank- but actual peace. The true peace that is a sense of calmness and assurance that you can only receive from God. The assurance that no matter what, everything will be ok. It was not until I totally submitted to the will of God and His purpose for my life that I received that peace. It was in that moment that I finally received what I was in search of and that is the peace that only He can give us.

Today, I challenge you to submit to God and His purpose for your life.
Peace be unto you.

MOMENTS OF MEDITATION

DAY TWENTY-FIVE

HE IS PREPARING ME

John 14: 1 - 3

Preparation prevents failure...

We live in a day and time of instant gratification. We have become a very inpatient society wanting what we want exactly when we want it! The longer we have to wait for what we want- the more irritable we become. The hypocrisy in this way of thinking is that we desire that everyone continue to be patient with us. Despite wanting everything at the snap of our finger- we still expect patience to be attributed to us. A common saying that I've always used is: "don't ask for what you don't give". This merely means that you shouldn't require from others, what you fail to extend in return. One aspect that I love about God is that He is so very patient with us. He continues to be patient with us even when we are impatient with Him. His patience also allows us to prepare for whatever He has in store for us. It is during the process of preparation and waiting that we learn more about Him and ourselves. I know that you desire all that He has for you immediately, but I guarantee if you allow Him to prepare you- you will maintain and appreciate all that He has for you even better.

Today, take some time to remember that every great meal has to be prepared before it is served. Our life with God is no different.

MOMENTS OF MEDITATION

DAY TWENTY-SIX

THE PROCESS OF PRODUCTIVITY

Psalm 1: 1 - 3

Be wise with your time...

Have you ever wondered why certain people are so successful, yet others are not? I have discovered that one's success is dependent upon many variables. One of the variables could be *who* we surround ourselves with. Another reason could be what we spend our time doing or how we utilize our time. These three aspects often play a critical role in the productivity within our lives. If you think about it, many of us spend our time on social media, watching television, or talking aimlessly on the phone about nothing important. Yet we wonder why our life isn't progressing the way that we want it to. The answer to this is simple. You really aren't being productive with your time. We all receive the same number of hours per day. The choices we make with our time affect how productive and successful we are. Starting today, you should create a weekly schedule that includes every hour of every day. Write down what you want to accomplish within that hour- and you will notice that by the end of that week, you will accomplish more than you ever have before.

Today, I challenge you to be productive with your time and your talents. For they are all a gift from God.

MOMENTS OF MEDITATION

DAY TWENTY-SEVEN

FORGIVE

Luke 6: 37

Forgive, because you have been forgiven...

One of the easiest, yet most difficult things for us as humans to do is forgive. We always want to be forgiven for our transgressions, yet we rarely want to forgive others. We often carry around hurt, pain, grudges, and disappointments for years simply because we refuse to forgive those that have hurt us. I have learned that when you forgive- it not only liberates the offender- it also liberates you from the bondage of the past. Total and absolute forgiveness allows you to be free. It allows you to move on from the past and start new. It allows you to enjoy the next moments in life that God has in store for us. Don't allow yourself to be held hostage by the past. Free yourself by forgiving anyone that may have hurt, harmed, or hindered you in the past. Forgive, so that your sins maybe forgiven while on your journey in life. The weight of unforgiveness can only be lifted by forgiveness. Imagine how our life would be if God never forgave us.

Today, take some time today to reflect on those that need your forgiveness. Imagine the weight that will be lifted once you truly forgive those that have hurt you.

MOMENTS OF MEDITATION

DAY TWENTY-EIGHT

ENDURE

Hebrews 6:15

Your goals are worth fighting for...

For most people, giving up is very easy to do. Giving up doesn't require great thought, it doesn't require one to have a strategy, and it certainly doesn't require support. All giving up requires is for one to decide to quit! Once you've made the decision just saying those words makes it your reality. However, there really is no reward when one decides to give up. You receive absolutely NOTHING when you make the decision to give up. It does, however, take a very strong person to endure a situation, as endurance requires strength, patience, and a sound mind. Unlike giving up, not everyone is equipped to endure and handle perseverance. This could be why quitting happens so often in our community. Enduring requires recognizing that it may not always be easy, but it is always necessary. The main difference between those that quit and those that endure is very simple. Those that endure always obtain or master their goal. Those that quit usually watch the goal ceremony from the crowd. Challenge yourself to commit to never giving up on your goals. For the reward is far greater for those that endure the journey.

Today, make the decision to endure,
and let those that quit admire you from the crowd.

MOMENTS OF MEDITATION

DAY TWENTY-NINE

LOVE

1 Corinthians 13: 1 - 8

Love is patient and love is kind...

Love is such a small word, but far stronger than all of the others. Love can cause a smile and in the same sentence, it can also cause one to come to tears. Love can make your day better and it can also make your day difficult. Love can make you feel joyous while also making you feel a pain unlike no other. Love can make you do things that you never thought you would do. Love has an elongated definition- yet, the word in itself is the definition. Everything that God has ever done was centered around love. His love for us is unending and without condition. While some see love as a noun, others see it as a verb. God certainly loves us with actions. Be grateful today, for even before we loved ourselves, God loved us. I love the Lord with all of my heart because He first loved me.

Today, pass love along to someone else,
as there is no greater gift, than the gift of love.

MOMENTS OF MEDITATION

DAY THIRTY

TELL THE TRUTH

Ephesians 4:15

Truth and honesty will never cost you a penny...

Throughout life, I have discovered that most people I've encountered experience some form of stress. Stress is the cause of many hidden health and psychological conditions. Stress can be the product of many factors and can affect anyone- no matter their health, financial status, or mindset. There is one underlying factor to most stress related issues and that factor is the lack of being truthful. Let me explain. Many of us are not truthful with ourselves or with others within our life. The lack of telling the truth can cause a plethora of negative situations and outcomes. However, being truthful can be healthy for us as this forms a release within our bodies and minds. Many of us carry the burden of hiding secrets. Not just our secrets- but the secrets that many others entrust us with. Those secrets weigh us down- affecting us mentally, physically, and emotionally, as they produce an unnecessary stress on our bodies.

Today, make the decision to be truthful in all that you do, as it will make your life less stressful. Less stress equals a healthier and vibrant you!